# TABLES OF CONTENT

# HONEY

# OUT OF

# LAMENTATION

## A SHORT STORY

**VINCENT C NWABUEZE**

## EPIGRAM

**Despair and disappointment are the parents of countless inspired, inspiring triumphant creations**

**Rasheed Ogunlaru**

## DEDICATION

**To Joan.**



## AUTHOR'S NOTE

**Chapter 1**

Nkem pushes the squeezed #500 note she has been holding in her hand into the outstretched right hand of the driver from the back seat of the Toyota corolla, as soon as the car sputtered to a halt. She pulls the side door car lock, pushes the door open and climbed down from the yellow branded taxicab. She hesitated for a moment to straighten the crumpled hem of her skirt, pulling it to her knee's length, then glances at her wristwatch. It is already 5.30 pm in the evening. She shrugs her shoulders, ruing how time had fleeted . She waited for a moment by the kerb and sprints across to the opposite side of the road when no vehicles were approaching. As she begins to saunter towards the giant gate of the popular and strategically located Berger Motor Park some meters away, her traveling bag slung across a shoulder, she for the umpteenth time reassures herself, that no matter the circumstance, she will be traveling

Presently, her mind went back to the last job interview she attended. It was a consulting firm- Mekas Consultants. She had applied for the post of receptionist, despite the fact that she is a graduate. After more than a dozen job interviews with her degree certificate without any positive result, she had learnt to lower the bar.

By the time she arrived, the whole place was filled with a large number of job applicants, that if a grain of pepper fruit had been



thrown into the air, it will find it difficult finding a place to rest on the floor. They were horded to a waiting room – a sparsely furnished room. By midday, she was called into the interviewing room.

‘ Young lady your name’ The elderly man with a receding hair line and dressed in a distinctive three- piece suit began immediate she sat at the chair facing him. The air in the large office space was cozy as an air conditioner hummed from a side of the wall.

‘Nkem ‘

‘So, what makes you think you are suited for this job you applied for?’ From the records in your file before me, you have a degree in political science.’ As he spoke, Nkem noticed that he was peering at the cleavages of her bosom through the rim gold plated eye glasses that sat on the bridge of his nose.

‘Sir I think I can fit in ‘

‘Ok, tell me something about the job routines ?’

‘Answering phone calls, maintaining files and document,--

‘Ok, the company will get back to you’

And this was some six months back and no news ever since then.

7

The Berger Motor Park is situated on the outskirt of the city center. As she walks through the pedestrian gate heading for the section where commercial buses are parked, she felt a gentle push at her left shoulder. She

turned to see who touched her. Standing before her is Nsofor, her former school mate and lover way back in their secondary school days.

‘Ha Nsofor ‘She shouted with excitement, grinning from ear to ear and spread her arms wide towards him. Both glued together like Siamese twins. For a moment, Nsofor felt the softness of her breasts as her nipples pressed warmly

on his chest, felt her racing heartbeats and perceived the odor of the cheap perfume she wore. Suddenly a wildfire of desire erupted from the base of his pituitary gland, sizzling gradually through the tiny

networks of his veins, before ending abruptly at the base of his groin area, setting his phallus on fire of love. Memories of their love making days came rushing back to him, and he wishes he would have her again.

’ Where are you heading to this evening Nkem?’ Nsofor began after they had disentangled from each other.

‘It is you I will ask?’ Nkem replied, giggling.

“But am the one that asked first. So, tell me.’ Nsofor said reaching for her right hand and squeezing her fingers tenderly in his palms.



‘Well dear I am traveling to Ahaba-my ancestral town at the heart of mid- western part of the country, some three thousand kilometers away.’

‘But don’t you think is late to do so this evening?’ It is already getting dark and dangerous to travel at this time’ Nsofor replied, a worried expression now hued on his face.

‘Well, it is not that I intentionally set out to travel this late. Dear, I am telling you the truth. Yes, you heard me right. You got to believe me. Can you believe I set off early at dawn for this journey to evade the city's chaotic traffic only to find myself in the park at this time of the day?' She said a vague expression sitting on her face.

Nsofor said nothing, but only nodded his head as Nkem continued to rattle on.

'Cars and trucks bleaching out grey suffocating smoke; carts that are filled with jerry cans of water and pushed by city urchins in dirty caftans, cold sweat dripping down their forlorn faces and putrid smell ensuing from their sweat filled armpits; the notorious ever busy city pick pockets who pretend they are just hawking articles-baby toys, belts, utensils- along the roadside, but are cunningly looking out for the slightest opportunity to pounce on personal effects in the cars of careless and unsuspecting motorists; All were trotting at snail pace and sometimes bumping at each. Dear, you need to experience this to understand what am talking about.'



'So, this was how I was held up in the monstrous Eko traffic for such a long time that at a point I had contemplated canceling my trip.'

'Dear but wait a moment. Yes, I know you would prefer I defer my travel till the next morning?'

Nsofor nods his head. 'Well, don't you think is the best thing to do?'

'No, I cannot. I am sorry to disappoint you. I must travel. This is because, the interview I am going for, which is coming up the next morning at exactly 9 am on the dot, is so important to me.'

'Dear, let me explain further why this journey is so important to me.'

'Is it not said "'He who feels the pain knows where it pinches him?"

'I have gone through a lot in this life brother. Can you believe this is my twelfth years after graduation from the university; Yes, an incredible four thousand, three hundred and eighty days; and another one year of compulsory service to my fatherland as a youth Corper, the popular acronym used to refer to Nigerian youths during their mandatory one-year intensive national youth service corps program, and eleven good years scouting for jobs.

'Frankly, I will confess though, there have been lots of job interviews I had attended over the years. But in the end, nothing comes out of it. Only promises here and there and the now familiar. '



"You will get back from us soon"

'This has become the usual ubiquitous mantra that I have learned to chant for a long time.'

'But most never cared to get back to me. And when it appears the gods have heard my supplication and decided to put smiles on my face by a way of a response from one of them informing me that my application has proceeded to the next and final stage, all will suddenly fizzle out and crumble like the proverbial pack of cards, when the channel of communication will suddenly go into an eternal mute.'

'To a point, I must confess I became delusional, and thoughts of suicide occasionally sneaking into my consciousness struggling to be birthed and becoming alive.'

‘I remember Chisom, my course mate in the university who I learnt committed suicide by drinking the local herb Otiapiapia mixed in water. I learned she could not bear the suffering and humiliation any longer after so many years of graduation and no job to keep body and soul running and meet the financial expectation of her poor parents who had spent so much to see her through the ivory towers. Poor soul.’

‘But is suicide the solution?’

Nsofor twirls his right hand over his head, gurgle his throat and spit out a



mouthful of sputum.

‘Never.’ He shouted. ‘Never my dear’

‘You see that is the reason I tell myself and anyone that cares to hear me out, that suicide is not the way out. I must hang on hope and believe that someday things will get better and turn out good. God, Chukwubinigwe -the one that resides in heaven, I know this is true.’ Nkem added raising her head toward the skies as if in supplication.

## Chapter 2

'Dear Nsofor, I know by now you are beginning to understand my predicament and where am coming from.'

' So just like the proverbial tortoise who fell into a deep ditch filled with feces when no one knew and had taken the incident as her fate, but a few days later, suddenly getting to the understanding that efforts are being made to rescue her from the quagmire, became desperate and impatient to exit the ditch, to the extent that she even started shouting that her rescuers should hurry up before she is suffocated by the stench of excreta inside the pit. '

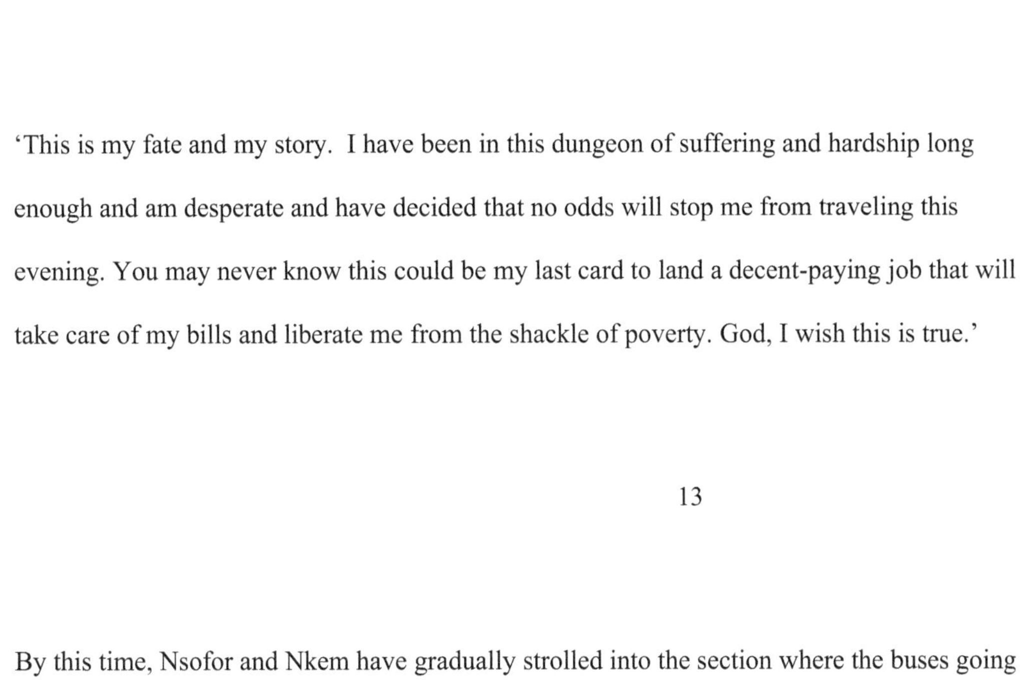

'This is my fate and my story. I have been in this dungeon of suffering and hardship long enough and am desperate and have decided that no odds will stop me from traveling this evening. You may never know this could be my last card to land a decent-paying job that will take care of my bills and liberate me from the shackle of poverty. God, I wish this is true.'

## 13

By this time, Nsofor and Nkem have gradually strolled into the section where the buses going east were loading, Nsofor's right arm over her shoulders.

## Chapter 3

The Berger motor park is expectedly filled with a cocktail of people who have congregated together for diverse purpose. There are travelers embarking on their journeys, traders struggling to earn a living who stood by their wares calling on passerby to patronize them, men, women, children, the disabled, beggars, madmen, mad women, preachers of the word, pickpockets, yes name them and I know even ghost entities. All were milling around.

And talking about ghost entities, Nkem presently felt goose pimple spread all over her hands as she called to memory the advice Adanee-her mother- gave her a long time ago after relieving one of those of her ghostly fantasy tales, when a neighbor reported her to her mother that she caught her playfully bending down with her head between her thighs to watch the people at Ogbeli market.

Her mother had said to her that evening as she sat beside the fireplace with her peeling the shell off the melon seeds, as the fire crackled away cooking their supper.



"My daughter, never you be so naughty to put your head in-between your legs in a crowded park or marketplace. Because, if you do, you will see-ndimoo- spirit entities that walk about without feet touching the ground and even those that walked with their heads."

"And God save you if you are not only rewarded with a vicious hard knock on your head for your mischief but also live to regret the rest of your life sorrowing thereafter"

As Adanee voice ricocheted in her head, she suddenly feels the aura of spirit entities lurking around and struggling with the living souls.

The din was something else. lord have mercy. It was like a drawn elastic band, which is approaching its breaking point. But despite the imminent approach of night fall, there is this calm amongst the   people. They continued their chores unpersuasively as if the approaching sunset will never come.

'Onitsha; Onitsha: one passenger remaining' She overhead a manly voice and turned towards the direction. The custodian of the voice is a burly built dwarf with scars on both sides of his cheeks. He wore a dirty torn and faded t-shirt which offers a revealing glimpse into his tick biceps that appears like those of a village wrestler, and on his waist, an equally faded jeans pants. On his head was a fez cap which was worn with the front side of the cap turned backwards. He keeps shouting at the top of his voice gesticulating now and again towards a minibus parked beside a pool of other commercial vehicles.

And just some distance from him, another individual, this time a lean and tall looking man, garbed in blazer shirt and jeans pants, a lighted cigarette stub wedged between his lip, was also shouting 'Aba, aba: just one seat remaining.'

'Darling, come along with me as I lead you into the interesting world of the city's motor park boys euphemistically known as the 'Ndiocho-ndinje' Nsofor whispered to her as they stopped beside one of the buses.

'Ndiocho-ndinje, - those that Hussle for passengers 'continued Nsofor in local parlance are motor park urchins.

'They are ubiquitous and powerful class of garage boys seen in most motor parks in our cities. Their job is to scout for passengers, making sure these passengers enter the designated vehicles they are loading, and ensuring that passengers' personal effects are safely kept in the trunk of the vehicles.'

'And because they are remunerated based on the number of passengers they source for the vehicles, in most cases these crops of urchins, out of overzealousness and greed and coupled with the

fact they want to make more cash, overload the vehicles with excess number of passengers.'

'Do they care?' Nsofor asked more to himself than to her.'Of course, they do not care. Just like the popular cliché in pidgin English "Wetin concern agberos with overload' what is the business of motor park urchins with regards to the comfort of the passengers, they care less.'

'Selfishly, they are preoccupied with lining their pockets with lucre. They are not troubled, nor bothered about the comfort of the passengers they serve.'

'And when they are not loading vehicles for the drivers that send them, they keep themselves occupied either drinking Aboh –a local type of concoction made from a cocktail of myriad of roots and ogogoro –our native local gin, while seated in the numerous make shift stalls that dotted the length and breadth of the park; or be smoking weeds and cigarettes; snatching bags of unsuspecting women and infamously gang-raping innocent ladies at dark alleys.'

Nkem shook her head in disbelief.

'Aunty, aunty you dey travel?' Nkem heard a male voice.

She turned to ascertain who was calling her aunty. Behold standing beside her was another of the motor park touts. This time, not these matured people, but a young man. He seems barely not more than twenty -one; tall, slim, clean-shaven, and handsome. She wondered what this one is doing here of all places.

'He ought to be at school' Nkem said, turning to face Nsofor.'Don't you think so?'



Nsofor nodded his head as if he is in agreement with her submissions.

The young man was dressed in boxer shorts and white sleeveless singlets and nothing more.

Turning back again towards the young person, NKem shakes her head and held firmly to her baggage because she knows that is the next thing he will want to do-take her baggage.

As she expected, he reached out to wrest the strap from her shoulder. He left her, sighed discontentedly, and goes after another target – an elderly woman who was walking towards them. Little boys and girls wearing dirty and crumpled dresses saunter about shouting on top of their voices and pestering people to buy edibles like oranges, bananas, biscuits, and iced cold sachet water in plastic and aluminum trays which they carried on their heads.

A little girl accosts Nkem and barely pushing her tray of oranges into her face.

'Aunty buy oroma suru-uso, sweet orange.'

'No, I won't'

'Aunty test and see very sweet orange' the girl continued still undaunted, picking one of the oranges in her hand and slicing it into two.

Nkem stood her ground and shrugs her shoulders again, a friendly mien perched on a side of her face.



After loitering around for a moment and seeing that Nkem was not in the mood to patronize her, moved on.

'Onitsha: Onitsha: 'one passenger still remaining' The burly one was still chanting his mantra.

His voice however has noticeably gone hoarse, obviously from the prolonged shouting it has been subjected to all evening. His chant tried unsuccessfully to subsume the unending din emanating from the crowd.

'Come let us go to that other bus. It seems that there a lot of passengers in it.' Nsofor said to her almost dragging her along.

They walked across a column of stores where fancy goods are displayed and got to where the bus was parked. It was a ten-seater HiAce bus. When they looked inside, they saw four women and four men were already seated. Nsofor enquired from the burly Agbero, and he pointed to a vacant seat by the window, next to a seat being occupied by a pregnant woman.

'Brother only one-person seat remains here 'he said pointing at the vacant seat.

'How much to Onitsha?'

'#2000 '

'She will pay #1000' Nsofor pleaded, a bit flushed at the high-pitched voice the



tout was addressing him despite the fact he was just a few steps away from where he was standing. Does he think he was deaf and cannot hear him clearly?

'No brother the fare is #2000." He insisted.

Nsofor whispered something to Nkem's ears, and both went to lean on the walls of one of the fancy stores. They wanted to know if he will reconsider and accept their offer.

And as expected, their mind game paid off. After a moment, the urchin crawled back to them and began speaking in a whisper in his usual pidgin English.

"Aunty ok Nwanyi marama. Fine lady I go just comot #500 for you' As he said this, he winked lewdly at Nkem.

Nkem smiled and was just starring at him. In her mind, she is imagining how shallow this class of people, the dregs of society reason. 'Must they toast any lady they come across.?'.

'But make you no tell other passengers say I collect dat kin amount from you oh. Dey fit vex if dey know.' He added finally, a faint smile playing on a side of his face, as if he were doing her a favor. He slouched closer to her, pushing his rugged face aggressively towards hers, and offering her a grin as his right hand goes for the strap of the bag on her shoulder. Immediately he did so, his breath hit Nkem like a thunderbolt. It reeked of alcohol and stench of weed all mixed together. She



saw the incisors in his upper jaw. Three were badly stained with cigarette tar and a center tooth was missing.

Nkem stepped backwards almost in horror. She brought out her purse, unzipped it and brought out some monies.

'Here Oyah take 'she said handing over three-five hundred-naira notes-into his outstretched hand.

'Thank ma god go bless you' He smiles as he collects the money, deep one of his fingers in his tongue, counted them, crumples it in his right palm as if he meant to squeeze the very life out of the lifeless piece of papers, and proceeded to put it quickly into the back of his jean's pocket.

Then he ran off to the back of the bus, opens the boot and placed her bag among the other passengers' luggage.

Nsofor stayed back outside beside the side window of the bus, while Nkem clambered inside the bus to occupy her seat by the window beside the pregnant woman. Not long, one of the men seated right at the rear of the bus, stoutly built with a protruding tummy and a scowl on his face, got up suddenly, exited the bus and moved towards the area where a pool of accidented vehicles were packed. As he stood beside one of the decrepit cars, he pretends he wanted to answer the call of nature as he fidgets with the fly zipper of his trouser.

## 22

Five minutes, twenty minutes and still counting the man was yet to return to the bus.

Nsofor caught the trick of the man. He goes to the side window and beckons on Nkem and whispers into her ears.

'That fellow that left the bus is not a genuine passenger, but rather one of those motor park touts humorously known as NDINOCHI.'

'Really' Nkem said, one of her brows raised in bewilderment.

'Yes, my dear.'' This is their stock in trade.' Nsofor said.

'In other to deceive intending travelers that the vehicles they boarded are already fully occupied and ready to take off, drivers of commercial buses devise a means by hiring the service of these motor park touts – NDINOCHI - placeholders for passengers. This class of motor park touts sit in various positions inside the vehicle like genuine travelers. They disembark one after the other as genuine passengers get into the buses, pretending they were going to ease themselves. But they never come back. Instead, it is new and genuine passengers that usually take their seats.'

Nkem was dumfounded. What could she or any of the passengers do? Nothing.

So down by one passenger, they began the long wait to get another replacement going to the east.

23

As they waited, she feels a pang of hunger in her stomach, and it just occurred to her that she had not eaten anything until now. Two competing thoughts vied for supremacy in her mind: The first suggested she gets down and look for a Buka- a foods stall where cheap cooked foods are sold by women with jutting buttocks and pudgy arms known as 'Mama put' in local parlance. But the other thought advice against doing so because the bus might leave her behind.

Through the side window, she hailed one of the young ones hawking edibles. In a moment, a dozen hands from the hawkers were forcing bananas, biscuits, bread, and all manner of edibles through the small, opened window of the bus. Nkem bought two packets of biscuits and a bottle of cold drink and settled down to devour her delicacy.

## Chapter 4

By the time they finally leave the city's motor park, the sun was making her final downwards slide towards the west of the city, her beautiful golden rays settling on the horizon in an unforgettable blaze of glory. The sight was soothing to the soul. Nsofor kept waving at her until he receded out of sight.

Nkem brings out her rosary beads as a devout catholic would do and begins to toll the strings of beads, offering prayers silently in her heart to saint Michael and other myriad of hosts of angels in heaven for a safe journey, and afterwards made the sign of the cross on her temple and chest. Done with the prayers, she brings out a paperback- a novel by Agatha Christie - and settles down to read some pages before darkness will set in.

As the journey progressed, her eyes oscillated between the pages of the novel she is reading, and the pregnant woman seated beside me.



She was a tall woman, round-faced with a permanent dimple on both cheeks and a swarthy complexion. She must have been a beautiful lady when she was younger as she still retains those delectable features even in her present condition. Her baby bump, which has grown big, bulged out from the tight gown outfit she was wearing like an inflated balloon begging to be set free from captivity. looking at her, it was obvious that she was in the last stage of her pregnancy, and soon would be due to deliver her baby.

Nkem began to ponder on why a woman in such a precarious condition has decided to embark on a suicidal journey as this one.

'If labor pains start in this forest, what will she tell her 'Chi [ guarding angels] '?

'Won't her ancestors blame her for acting so foolishly?'

Just then as if reading her thoughts, the woman started to moan, clawing tenaciously on Nkem's right wrist squeezing them so hard as if they were the cause of her pains.

Then Nkem felt a cold sensation on her right foot. When she looked down, she saw a clump of dark liquid on the portion of the floor where the pregnant woman was sitting which was gently spreading all over the whole place. Obviously, without doubt, these were the water from her body- a clue that the baby inside her tummy was on the way-due for delivery.

By now, darkness has completely set in. They bus is cruising through the dark lonely road, which is only minimally illuminated by the light from their vehicle's headlamp and intermittently from the strands of light that emit from the headlamp of oncoming vehicles. And sandwiched on either side, are column of forest of trees that seemed like tall ghoulish creatures.

'Driver the pregnant woman seated here with me is about to give birth oh:' Nkem shouted in panic, almost crouching from her seat for her voice to be heard, when the clawing from the woman's fingers became unbearable and persistent.

Heads swung towards our direction. But the driver who let out a sigh of grudge, never wanted to stop, not until the male passengers harangued him and he hit so hard on the break that everyone was pushed forward.

Slowly, the bus eventually veered off the road and stopped by the sidewalk.

There was calm in the air, but amidst this calm, floated the intermittent noise made by crickets, crows and the croaking of frogs.

Occasionally, one could see fireflies as they fly around with the blinking poor lights that trail their movement.

Luckily two or three passengers who had phones that were equipped with torch lights came to our rescue and switched them on. We began to disembark from the bus. Nkem held the pregnant woman on her arms and with a tender manner lead her out of her seat and they came out of the bus.

Two of the women brought out their lappa and spread them on the wet grass a little distance from the bus and the pregnant woman laid on it, while more of the lappa brought out by the other women were used to form an emergency 'labor 'room cubicle thereby veiling the men's preying eyes.

The three women went to work on the pregnant woman. One parted her legs, while the other two women held her hands, one on her right arm and the other on her left arm.

'Oya push 'the tall fair-complexioned woman spoke gently to the pregnant woman in Ibo language, encouraging her to push hard to facilitate quick delivery.

'Ehwo Nnem oh nyeram aka 'the pregnant woman howled hysterically in agony as she summoned the benevolent help of her ancestors.

'I say push harder woman' her voice suddenly turned gruffy and sat on the wings of a stale wind that swept across the neighborhood. Then calmly, she ran her fingers expertly on her inflated belly and along the pelvis region of her hip, tapping then softly, here and there like a trained midwife would do.

The head of the baby pushed out.



'Push harder, harder' the woman encouraged her.

The pregnant woman summoned the last vestige of energy in her, screamed and passed out

The fair-complexioned woman expertly held the trunk of the baby and pulled gently until the baby was completely out of the mother's vagina and with a razor blade cut off the umbilical cord. The baby remained dumb. The woman hit the motionless baby slightly at one of the shoulders and suddenly, a shrill cry pierced through the forest, re-echoing far into the forest. Guess what? It was the cry of the newborn.

While she carried the baby away wrapped in a lappa and placed on her bosom, the other women went about cleaning up the new mother.

Soon, the atmosphere turned into a carnival as the women begin to sing and dance in a circle thanking the giver of life for the birth of another beautiful soul.

Welcome to our world baby.

The End.





**EDITORIAL REVIEW**

Vincent Nwabueze studied sociology and law. He began writing while still a college student. His works have appeared in The Society Voice Project, the Voices Project, Amazon platform and the first edition of this story was first published in the Preservation foundation Inc. One of his short stories was shortlisted at the 2020 African Writers Awards. His debut novel manuscript has just been completed.

www.ingramcontent.com/pod-product-compliance
Lightning Source LLC
LaVergne TN
LVHW010513160826
845677LV00012B/2825

* 9 7 9 8 3 5 5 2 0 0 3 8 1 *